Gun T RPO Organization Guide

Copyright: Kenny Simpson
All Rights Reserved
ISBN Number: 978-1-7351591-3-3

Introduction

 # Introduction

I, like most coaches, have worked hard to listen to people I respect and attempt to take little nuggets from those willing to give. Now I have the opportunity to give back, and I hope this offensive system can be of help to you in your journey as a coach. Feel free to take any part of this offense that can help you, but I feel what makes it work is the entire system.

We have worked hard to continue to grow it and work through the problems that can come from blending different worlds.

The entire system can be found on coachtube.com:

There is also more information on my website: FBCoachSimpson.com.

This book is also the 3rd in a series of books that can be found on Amazon or FBCoachSimpson.com.

 # Introduction

This book is an organizational supplement to the Gun T RPO offensive system. The plan in this book is to go through how to organize your staff, build practice plans, build game plans, call a game in this offense and other duties that are needed.

I am very appreciative of the support and in no way do I have all the answers. However, I have learned a few things along the way, and I hope some of them can help you in your journey. This offense has been very good to me, and I hope to see it help other coaches.

Recommendations

Quotes

"Coach Simpson's offensive system is simply one of the best out there. Coach does a phenomenal job of explaining his offense in detail. I've always been a power spread coach but there was just something about this system that made me want to learn more. This is truly the best of both worlds in the wing-t and spread blended together. This season we took over a program that had been spread the last three years with a division 1 QB, and two division 1 WRs. We were taking over a team that returned 1 TD from the year before and no offensive starters. We decided to install this offense with almost no summer install work and ended up averaging over 30 points and just over 350 yards per game. Lastly, this system is very adaptable to fit your kids strengths year in and year out. I highly recommend checking out Kenny Simpson's Gun-T Offense." - Coach Lucas Stanton

"Coach Simpson has done it again. Our staff has used his previous material and have become better coaches for it. Coach Simpson's ability to break complex concepts into smaller parts is excellent. His material is perfect for any coach that wants to become better at his craft." – Coach Joel Brose

Quotes

"Coach Simpson's Gun T Offensive Overview is an excellent offensive resource. This course provides the foundation of Coach Simpson's offensive philosophy. Coach believes in the monikers that "Less is More" and the "Rule of 3", which both were evident in the explanation of the offense. His explanations were clear and concise, and the presentations were easy to follow." - Todd Knipp

"This is absolutely amazing. Coach Simpson does an excellent job of explaining his system. Whether you're a young coach or an experienced coach this is must see. You can easily see why he is a successful coach. His detailed organization is on point and I cannot wait to learn more from Coach Simpson." - Mike Kloes

"I've been following coach Simpson for a while now and it's very clear to me that even though I may not be a HC, we have similar philosophies. If you are a Wing T guy looking for ways to "Modernize" your offense, or a Spread guy looking for an effective and efficient run game this is the offense you should be looking at!" - Coach Sheffer

 # Quotes

"Most offensive systems you must have really good players to run them, but with Coach Simpson's 'Gun-T' RPO system, you can be very successful just manipulating defenses with the X's & O's." - Steven Swinson, Indiana Weslyian University

"As a traditional wing T coach for over 30 years I was looking for a package to add to my offense in order to force defense's to defend width and depth. Coach Simpson's Gun-T RPO offense does exactly that with the built in "what if then" RPO's and RRO's." - Coach Brissette

"The Gun T RPO System really helped us evolve our wing T offense and really put defenses in conflict. This system helped us break a 20 game losing streak and finish with a winning record for the first time since 2014." -Tom Mulligan, Head Coach Elmwood Park High School, Elmwood Park, New Jersey

Table of Contents

Implement the Gun T	13
-Personnel	15
-Timeline	23
-Organize your Staff	33
Practice Organization	53
-Practice Theory	54
-Practice Schedules	59
-Individual Time	70
-POD Work	75
-Team and Situational Football	81
Formations/Wrinkles	83
Opponent Prep	111
Build a Call Sheet	115
Tempo	123
If-Then	127
Conclusion	135

Implementing

 # Implementing

I get asked often how to "put this system in" or other variations of how to install the Gun T RRO System. The answer is complicated – so I have decided to break it into multiple parts as a coach.

1) Personnel – Make sure you find the players needed and put them in the right positions. Players win games. As a coach our job is to put them in a place that matches their skill set.

2) Timeline – Where do I start? What goes in first? How much time should I spend? As a coach the answer always seems the same – "it depends". Each situation is unique. I am giving a general guide, but as a coach I try to make sure we are very good at what we are doing before advancing. So spend more time if needed.

3) Building a staff. How to use your coaches? Who coaches where? If you are a head coach or an offensive coordinator, your job is now going to be dependent on those assistant coaches.

Personnel

Personnel Choices

When you are designing any offense it should always adapt and evolve to your players' skill sets. While I love certain plays, each season our "best" play rotates depending on what our personnel looks like. Working with scheme is fun, but football is not played on a whiteboard and your X's may be better or worse than their O's at certain skills. The great offensive coaches are always able to highlight the skill set of their players and hide their deficiencies as much as possible.

In this section, I will give you the "optimal" skills each position has. Understand that if you do not have each position, you can still run the system, but I'd recommend highlighting specific parts. I refer to a few of those in the "IF-THEN" section later in this book.

As a coach be sure to constantly evaluate your players and find their strengths. In the Gun-T RPO system there are multiple spots that can have different skill sets, but a few key ones that you want to place your "better" players.

Personnel Choices

When running this offense there are a few "non-negotiable" parts you absolutely must have, but most of the time there are players with the required skills at each position. As coaches we must adapt our offense to the players we have. That being said there are a few qualities you should search for at each position.

Quarterback - This is the key to your offense. Ideally, this position would be a dual threat. While not everyone has that option, he must be at least able to pull the ball from time to time at the very least. The offense will drastically adapt to his skill set. If he is a thrower, the system has multiple passing schemes/play action and of course RPO plays. If he is a runner there are several designed runs for him, and the ability to go Empty is a must in today's game.

In short, find your best athlete that can handle the pressure of playing QB and adapt to what he does well. If given the option, I've always deferred to the guy that can run the ball and use his legs over a traditional QB. However, you can be successful with both.

Personnel Choices

F - This should be your best athlete. By design this position will touch the ball the most of any spot (except the QB position). It is easy to get them the ball in space (empty/screens) or simply run the ball (buck/belly). As with every position, you must adapt to their skill set, but this needs to be your best player.

B - This is the hardest position to find and the most important one. It will cause you to adjust what you do offensively to fit his skill set. Attempt to find your second best player, and if he is able/willing to block, put him in this position. Size will matter at this spot, since he will be asked to down block defensive ends and linebackers. If he is gritty, but undersized there are some adjustments that can be made, but he must be effective at blocking.

The second part of his job is as important. We want this player to be a good runner – if he is very athletic we will run jet and counter with him. He also needs to be able to catch at least short passes or play action passes. In my opinion, other than the QB, this position will dictate how much you use certain formations and plays.

Personnel Choices

A – A traditional slot WR. Often for us this is our third RB or an undersized WR. You can get him the ball on multiple concepts and even hand him the ball if you need to.

X – Traditional WR. Depending on what you have available, this position can be utilized often or not much.

Y – Tight-end. Must be able to block defensive lineman. His job is crucial on buck. We generally pick our 3rd guard for this spot. If he has the ability to catch the ball that is great, but he must be a willing and able blocker for this offense to work.

QG – Most important lineman on the team. He needs to be your most athletic player on the line. Size is secondary. He will be pulling on almost all strong side runs. When you decide who goes where, start at this position.

SG – Second most important lineman on the team. He will pull kick most of the time, but needs to be athletic enough to wrap for Quick Belly. Usually the stronger, not as athletic of the two guards.

Personnel Choices

QT – Next most important lineman. What his skill set brings to the table will allow you (or not) to run to the quick side and all your RPO game on the backside. He also needs to be able to get in space on screen and get to second level on RPO game.

C – Must be very consistent at snapping for the offense to run smoothly. Usually this is a smart kid that can call the fronts and is able to handle backside blocking. If he is not as great a blocker, we can give help, but if he is a solid blocker it makes the scheme much easier to achieve.

ST – Usually this is a very physical, but not as athletic tackle. Often for us this is our biggest lineman. If he played at the college level he would have to play guard since often these types of bodies struggle with speed. Must be able to down block, double team and cut/hinge on backside runs.

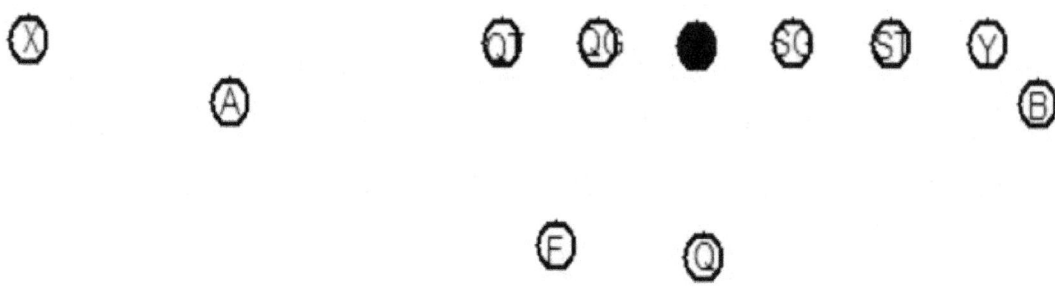

Personnel Choices

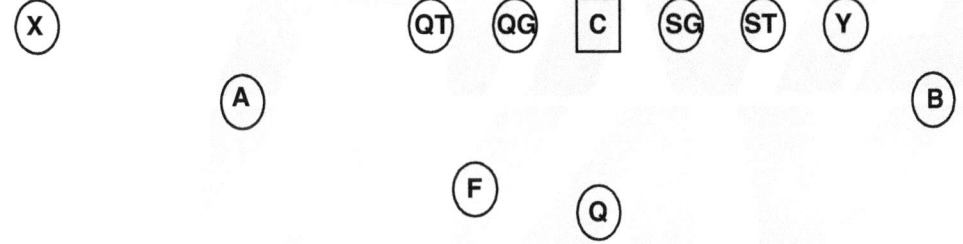

Position	Alignment
X	Top of the numbers
A	Split X and QT off the ball
F	Heels on QB toes. Split the QG and QT
Y	Head even with hip of center. 2 ft splits
B	2x2 off Y
QT	Head even with hip of center. 2 ft splits
QG	Head even with hip of center. 2 ft splits
C	On Ball
SG	Head even with hip of center. 2 ft splits
ST	Head even with hip of center. 2 ft splits
Q	Heels at 5 yards

Timeline

Install Schedule

The Gun T RPO system is a "series based" offense. That means that each play builds off of each other. This is very much in the Wing-T world. It also has much of its roots in the RPO world. The goal is to make one play concept many by blending them together. This makes installing the Gun-T not as difficult as many of the play concepts build and steal from each other.

To begin installing, you must decide how much time until the first game. Working backwards, I'd recommend 2-3 weeks to get the basic plays and RPO system installed. In this section I will share how I had 5-weeks until our first game at my most recent job. This forced a very speedy installation.

My recommendation would be to install the system out of the base set, before working formations/shifts. This allows for focus on the basics. In the next segment I will share a practice schedule form that shows our basic practice plan. We will work on rotating which "series" we are installing that day – usually by the day of the week.

Install Schedule

Series that need to be installed:

1) Buck series
   - Buck
   - Counter
   - Waggle
   - Buck Pass

2) Belly series
   - Belly
   - RPO Game
   - Any Influence game or "no pull runs"

3) Jet series
   - Jet
   - Quick Belly
   - Rollout Passing Game
   - Draw (Belly)

RPO's and Quick game work for Buck/Belly and can be installed day 1. As you read through this guide you will see that most RPO's only involve the QB/QT and WR's.

I'd recommend working different days of the week on each. Also pairing Jet Series with any Trips game helps speed along the passing concepts.

Install Schedule

This is a general practice plan we have for installation. We work a "series" during individual time, then the passes off that series in period 15-16, then the run attached during inside period. For example, if we were working our "belly series" we would cover an RPO attached during individual/pod and team. During pass period we would work quick game, or the screens attached.

There are more practice plans later in the book, but this is our general formatting. We would also steal time in period ¾ for the OL/QB for any explaining that needed to take place.

PD	QB	T	Y/B	X and A	OL	DL	ILB	OLB	DB	
1	SPECIALTY PERIOD --- DC with Non-specialty defensive players --- OL Coach with all linemen not involved									
2	Coach With Kicker, Coach With PAT Group, Coach With Punter/Snapper, Coach With Returnmen									
3	SPECIAL TEAMS GROUP - ROTATE THROUGH MAIN 4 -- Steal time for QB/OL -- Steal time for DL/ILB or DB/OLB									
4										
5										Crossover
6										
7	BREAK					BREAK				
8										Indy/Pod
9										
10										
11										
12	BREAK					BREAK				
13	1's on 1's - 5 minute offense vs. our defense, 5 minute offense working cards									1 on 1s
14										
15	1 on 1's PASS PERIOD					1 on 1's INSIDE PERIOD				
16										
17	BREAK PERIOD					DEFENSIVE PERSONELL GROUPINGS				Defense groupings
18	OFFENSIVE PERSONNELL OR SPECIALS					BREAK PERIOD				Offense groupings
19	Situational Offensive Period (TEAM)					Situational Defensive Period				Vs. Scout group
20										
21										
22	BREAK									
23	CONDITIONING									
24										

Install Schedule

At my most recent school, I had about five weeks to get our offense installed. The following pages are our first seven practice goals and what I was focusing on for each position group.

Each school can be different as far as a timeline is concerned. The main goal is to attempt to become great at the base plays/concepts and work to rep them as many times as possible.

New wrinkles are great, and we work to add them in as quickly as our athletes can handle them. However, we must be great at the basics first. As a coach we must constantly adapt to how quickly our athletes can handle concepts.

My advice would be to go slower than you think you must. It is always easier to come back later and add simple adjustments than to have to re-teach a basic concept that is a foundational piece.

*By the end of the seven days we were able to:
1) Line up in most of the formations I planned to run
2) Each position knew his tag to motion
3) Run all our base run plays and RPO game concepts
4) Had much of our quick game, screen game and play action game installed
5) Get into personnel groupings if we wanted ("Pro")

Install Schedule

Day 1 -
Formation period and rules - Red/Blue (flop, empty)
Motion period - "Fly"
Base run play - Buck
RPO/Screen - Fast Screen
Play Action - Waggle
QT - Base and "Steal"
OL - Buck, Rock/Load

Day 2 -
Formation period and rules - Red/Blue (Trips)
Motion period - "Bus"
RPO/Screen - Bubble and "stick"
Base run play - Jet and Quick Belly
Pass concept - Quick game - Smash
Play Action - Buck Pass
QT - Q Belly and Jet difference
OL - Quick Belly, Rodeo/Lasso

Day 3 -
Formation period and rules - Multiples (Empty-Flop and Flex-Flop)
Motion period - "Train"
Base run play - Strong Belly
RPO/Screen - Peak
Play Action - Waggle
QT - Base and Read
OL - Belly, Rock/Load

Install Schedule

Day 4 -
Formation period and rules - Red/Blue
Motion period - All
Base run play - Counter
Pass Concept - Verticals, F Slow screens
Quick Game - Out-Go and Out-Curl
OL - Counter, Slow Screen

Day 5 -
Formation period and rules - Flop
Base run play - Buck/Counter
Play Action - Waggle and Buck Pass
Single Routes - Single Routes
Verticals - Switches and Tags
QT - Rodeo/Lasso, Jail
OL - Buck/Counter, Rodeo/Lasso, Rock/Load

Day 6 -
Formations period and rules - Empty
Motions - "Fly"
Base run play - Q Run game (buck/belly/quick belly/q jet)
RPO - Peak, Bubble, Fast (all)
QT - Steal
OL - DUO

Install Schedule

Day 7 -
Formation period - Red/Blue Strong
Motions - "Fly"
Base run play - Belly Read, Q counter (read), Q Strong Belly
RPO - Screens (fast/bubble)
Pass play -
QT - "Read"
OL - Run game review, Pass protection

This is an example of our practice schedule we used during install days. Notice we went one way, so it may need to adapt to those who use two-way players. I have a full section on practices later in this book.

PD	QB	T	Y/B	X and A	OL	DL	ILB	OLB	DB	
1	SPECIALTY PERIOD --- DC with Non-specialty defensive players --- OL Coach with all linemen not involved									
2	Coach With Kicker, Coach With PAT Group, Coach With Punter/Snapper, Coach With Returnmen									
3	SPECIAL TEAMS GROUP - ROTATE THROUGH MAIN 4 -- Steal time for QB/OL -- Steal time for DL/ILB or DB/OLB									
4										
5										Crossover
6										
7	BREAK					BREAK				
8										Indy/Pod
9										
10										
11										
12	BREAK					BREAK				
13	1's on 1's - 5 minute offense vs. our defense, 5 minute offense working cards									1 on 1s
14										
15	1 on 1's PASS PERIOD					1 on 1's INSIDE PERIOD				
16										
17	BREAK PERIOD					DEFENSIVE PERSONELL GROUPINGS				Defense groupings
18	OFFENSIVE PERSONNELL OR SPECIALS					BREAK PERIOD				Offense groupings
19	Situational Offensive Period (TEAM)					Situational Defensive Period				Vs. Scout group
20										
21										
22	BREAK									
23	CONDITIONING									
24										

 # Formations

I have an entire section for formations in each book because I believe they give the "flavor" for the Gun-T system. With that being said, I would suggest working base plays and RPO's before working to become exotic with formations. Here is how I structure formation installation:

Red-Blue:	First week
Red-Blue Flop:	First/Second week
Red-Blue Empty:	Second week
Red-Blue Lion/Roar:	Second/Third Week
Other formations:	Fourth/Fifth Week

I start with "bus" motion the first week as well. When installing the Jet series it is natural to work this motion.

"Train" and "Fly" motion will come as you install "Flop" and "Empty" sets.

Since I was rushed to install the offense last season, you can see I worked much quicker (it also helps that I am much more comfortable with this offense). It can be sped up, but usually is best to go slow with formations.

 # Formations

Red
Red Flop
Red Lion
Red Empty
Red Flop Empty
Red Pro
Red Flex
Red Mustang

This is an example of each formation. If you'd like more detail refer to the Gun-T-Playbook. I also have a smaller section later in this book.

Building Your Staff

Coaching Choices

How you use your assistant coaches is key on all football staffs, but in this offense there are a few adjustments that can be made to help if you have a large or short staff. Here are the positions that it would be optimal to have a position coach for – **in a perfect world, here is how I'd set up my staff**:

OL – 2 coaches. One coach would handle Centers and Tackles and one would handle our guards. They could work with each other during install and separate out for pod work with one coach specializing in pulls and blocking in space and the other on down blocking and first level blocks.

TE – 1 coach. This player needs to be coached as an OL and a WR.

B – 1 coach. Again a versatile player that needs to be coached up well.

WR's – 1 coach. Can work with A and X in this offense with one coach.

QB – 1 coach. Usually the OC or HC.

RB – 1 coach. This position can be grouped with the QB or B coach if needed.

This is the best way to organize your staff if you have enough coaches. In the next pages I will give ideas on how to work with:

6 Coaches
5 Coaches
4 Coaches
3 Coaches
2 Coaches

Coaching Choices

If you have 6 coaches on offense, here is how to order them:

OL – 2 Coaches
QB – 1 Coach
TE – 1 Coach
RB/B – 1 Coach – B can work with TE coach for blocking
WR – 1 Coach

If you have 5 coaches on the offense, here is how to order them:

OL – 2 Coaches
QB/RB – 1 Coach – Can use position coaches for RB for pod work
TE/B – 1 Coach – Can use position coaches for B for pod work
WR – 1 Coach

If you have 4 coaches on offense, here is how to order them:

OL – 1 Coach – Will use other coaches for pod work
QB/RB – 1 Coach
WR – 1 Coach
TE/B – 1 Coach

Coaching Choices

If you have 3 coaches on offense, here is how to order them:

OL – 1 Coach
QB/WR/RB – 1 Coach – Can work RB/QB with the B coach in POD work.
TE/B – 1 Coach

If you have 2 coaches on offense, here is how to order them:

Lineman/TE – 1 Coach
Skill Players – 1 Coach

*This limits work that can be done, but you can still be creative in pod work to maximize drill time.

Weekly Schedule

Weekly Schedule

Setting a general schedule for your program is a must. Once install is completed and most of the offense is installed, staying organized is key to make sure that you are working the skills/plays needed each week. On the next page I have put a sample of a "typical" week for our program.

Key elements to make sure you are working:

-Individual skills needed

-Series based plays

-Situational football

Weekly Schedule

Individual skills needed: It is best to break this down by day to insure you are working each skill.

Series based plays: Again, I attempt to work these on different days of the week in the off-season and early season. Working one series on Monday, another on Tuesday the third on Wednesday with a blend/special plays on Thursday will make sure you are working the entire offense. As the season goes on, I try to do this during individual time and during team switch to situtational football.

Situational football: Being sure to schedule in time for 3rd downs, red zone, hash work, backed up, two and four-minute offense is key. This for us is usually always done during team periods. Setting a day of the week to insure you cover these scenarios is key.

Practicing Structure

Structure your days of the week so that you can get each situation you may face – Here is what we do on offense and defense each day:

Monday – Base plays, adjustments, game plan adjustments, 3rd/4th and shorts, installs

Tuesday – Hash work, Red zone work, 3rd and longs, 2 Minute drill

Wednesday – Short yardage, Gimmicks, Special Formations, 4 Minute drill
*Other defensive looks in individual and pod time (not in team)

Weekly Schedule

Typical Week

Sunday: Defensive staff meeting during the afternoon on Sunday to finalize gameplans
  3PM – 5PM
Coaching meeting (All coaches) at 7:00PM - 9:00PM
  - Go over grades
  - Pass out gameplans
  - Players of the week
  - Practice schedule

  All coaches need to have film graded by meeting

Monday: Lift: 2:30-2:50 --
Film: 2:55-3:15 – Opponent upcoming (defense) / Offense watch "fixes" needed
Awards: 3:20-3:35 – (POG – O, D, K, Scout and hand out all stickers)
Practice: 3:45-4:55

*JV Kids will leave for game if needed earlier and practice may be moved up if needed
- Go over mistakes on both sides in individual and then move on
- Special Teams: Work on any new adjustments
- Offense: Work on 1st and 10's and any formations/adjustments
- Defense: Go over main 5-6 formations and plays/tendencies and learn all keys
- Staff meeting for 20 minutes -- If no JV Game -- If JV (Edwards/Gould/Weaver go)

Tuesday: Lift: 2:30-2:55 --
Opponent film: 2:55-3:10
Meet in position groups: 3:10 – 3:20
Practice: 3:30-5:45
Staff meeting for 10 minutes

Wednesday: Lift: 2:30 – 2:55 -- Make-up lifts (JV), Film for SH
Practice film: 3:00 – 3:15 (Of Tuesday Practice in Team)
Practice: 3:25-5:30
Work on Goal Line offense and Goal Line defense
Work on 4 minute offense and "have to strip" defense

Thursday: No Lift
Practice film: 2:30 – 2:45 (Of Tuesday Practice in Team)
Meeting in positions: 2:45-2:55
INDO time: 3:05-3:20
  3:20 – 4:00: "Play the game" practice (early release)
Equipment check in locker room (Game uniforms in each locker) - Managers
QB's and Simpson/Gould meet for 20 minutes to finalize call sheets

Friday: Gameday - Do a "walk-through" for all players that may play – lifting JV only kids

Saturday: On own to grade players (due by Sunday night)

Weekend Schedule

Weekend Schedule

One of the questions each coach must answer is how they will handle preparation for the week. I am a big believer in allowing our athletes to have the weekends off if at all possible. We have brought groups in on Sunday afternoons to go through film on occasion when we were going to be limited on time on Monday, but in general I like to allow our athletes time to recover from the game.

With all the technology in today's society I think allowing coaches to work from home one day a week (usually Saturday) is a great thing. I give my coaches a list of expectations for their personal film breakdown and allow them to do this from home on Saturday.

Sunday afternoon and evening is when I bring my staff in to meet. For our offensive staff we have several goals, which are listed on the last page of this section. As a Head Coach much of my time is spent with the coordinators, and I have listed a sample schedule on the next page.

Being sure to maximize time on the weekend is key. Although some coaches enjoy being around the field house, I want to make sure we are working quickly and thoroughly to give those wishing to be with their families the option to do so.

Weekend Schedule

This is what my Sundays look like as a head coach. As you can see, most of this is team oriented, so the offensive scouting must be done on Saturday. What topics need to be handled inside the offense is listed on the following page.

Coaches come in at 1 PM to finish any work they have not done already
- Grading Players
- Scouting Opponent
- Meeting with Offensive/Defensive Staff Members
- List of Drills needed for the week
- Depth Chart and Ideas on Building Depth at Position or Personnel Changes Needed

Schedule
- Simpson meet with DC - 1PM
- Simpson meet with SP Teams - 2PM
- Simpson meet with Trainer 2:30PM
- Players get therapy 2-3PM with Cody
- Defensive staff meeting during the afternoon on Sunday to finalize gameplans 2PM – 5PM
- Offensive staff meeting during the afternoon on Sunday to finalize gameplans 1PM - 5PM
- Pick up waters at Harps 3:45 PM
- Pick up meal at Sonic 4:00 PM
- Break for any evening church or family time 5:00 PM-7:00 PM
- Coaching meeting (All coaches) at 7:00PM - 9:00PM
    - Go over grades
    - Pass out gameplans
    - Players of the week
    - Practice schedule
        - ****All coaches need to have film graded by meeting****

Weekend Schedule

Offensive Weekend Schedule:

Offensive Breakdown:
- HUDL Input
- Simpson: ODK all games, highlights off our games
- Denton: Play call of our games
- Smith: Down and Distance, Hash and any other needed inputs of our games
- Scouting
- Edwards: Oppositions plays
- ALL: TOTAL BREAKDOWN OF OPPONENT

Gameplan goals:
Understand defensive front -- Attacking or Reading, Learn keys of defensive players
Find players to attack and avoid
How will they line up to main sets
How good are DB's/OLB's in space -- Who won't hit

Scouting Opponents for Offense

What to do with your game plan based on opponents
- Coverage checks and Passing game tweaks
- When is the best time to take a shot on offense – and at who?
- When do they go "goal line"
- Who to attack and who to avoid?
- What will they key on your offense – can you do false keys/tendency breakers?

*This is our Coaching checklist

Game Duties

 # Game Duties

Game management is key for any offense to succeed. It is no different in the Gun T RPO system. With many states and schools moving to a sideline replay system (which I'd highly recommend) it has become much easier to make adjustments. To do this requires some organization on the front end. Here is a list of items that need to be set before a game:

1) Who will handle adjustments on the sideline? If this is not you, it must be someone that you trust and is capable of seeing the offense.

2) Rotational jobs. This can be delegated, but needs to be discussed as to who is to be in the game. The last thing you want is to call a play when the player you need has been rotated off the field.

3) Calling plays and communicating them. Many ways to do this. I purposefully did not tell how we do it as we will change it each season, but it needs to be practiced.

4) Charting the game. I usually delegate this to a coach in the box. They keep a touch chart as well as other areas I want them watching.

Game Duties

Sideline Management

General Guidelines:
1. Only Coach Simpson will speak with and deal with officials. If you have a concern let him know.

2. Remain calm on the sideline so that our athletes will follow our lead. Energy is great, but we need steady adjustments and to be a calming influence on our athletes.

3. Remember you represent our school. No one wants to lose, but if we expect our athletes to remain under control we must also.

Coaches Roles

Simpson - Time management, Game management, Overall management. While each coach will be responsible for their groups, Coach Simpson has final say on all personnel or scheme decisions.

DC - Defensive calls, adjustments and personnel. Will use TV while offense is on the field.

DL - Defensive line rotation, adjustments. Kickoff, Punt Return and XP/FG Block Teams. Will assist in monitoring the sideline while offense is on the field.

DB - Defensive backs rotation, coverage calls, adjustments. Will be with TV while offense is on the field.

OLB - Outside linebackers rotation, adjustments. KOR, Punt, XP/FG Team. Will assist in monitoring the sideline while offense is on the field.\

OSkill - Offensive skill rotations, adjustments and personnel. Will use the TV while the defense is on the field. Gameplan management and notes for adjustments.

OL - Offensive line rotations, adjustments and personnel. Will use the TV while the defense is on the field.

Box Offense - Have offensive gameplan in the booth. Assist with adjustments as needed.

Box Defense - Have defensive gameplan in the booth. Assist with adjustments as needed.

Coaching Organization

The following pages are some sample forms of what I use to organize my staff. They are not unique to the Gun-T offense, but should help some with organizing your staff. I have found that X's and O's are very important, but if a staff is not organized, much of the time will be wasted getting set up.

Feel free to use (or not) any of these guides for:
Halftime organization
Pre/Post Practice
Game day set up.

Coaching Organization

Half Time Organization

Things that must take place during half time:
1. Players must be given time to rest.
2. All injury and equipment problems taken care of.
3. Staff must analyze the first half and make plans for the second half.
4. Players must be re-motivated to play the final and most important part of the game.

Halftime divided into four periods:

1. First period (four minutes).
    1. Staff meetings.
    2. Team rest.
    3. Injury and equipment care.

2. Second period (four minutes).
    1. Offense and Defensive position coaches meet with assigned groups.

3. Third period Offense and defensive Coordinators meet with their entire offense or defensive squads. (Four minutes).

4. Fourth period (four minutes)
    1. Head coach meets with both offense and defense as a team.
    2. Return to field for warm-up.

In order to stay on schedule we will assign a staff member to keep meeting times on schedule. One coach or manager will be responsible for keeping the time as well as letting the head coach know how much time is left before the start of the second half.

Coaching Organization

Pre-Practice Responsibilities

Dummies: White/English

Cones: White/English

Footballs: Long/White

Water: Ashburn

Timer: Weddle

Film equipment: Long/Weddle

Post-Practice Responsibilities

Footballs/Water/Dummies/Cones: Same

Film onto Hudl: Long

Discipline players: Simpson/English

Lock-up: See List

*See calendar for staying until all players are gone

Coaching Organization

Home Game-Day Duties

Chain set/Blow-up helmet/Field Markers/Pylons:

Water/Injury Ice: Trainer (Ashburn confirm)

Headsets: Weddle

Whiteboards/Sideline seats: White

Camera Charge: Long

Pre-game Meal: Simpson/Mom's Squad

Greet Refs: Simpson

Greet Visitors: McCoy

Gameballs: Long

Injury kit/taping: Trainer (Ashburn confirm)

Stats: Assigned for each side of the ball

Offensive gameplan: White

Defensive gameplan: McCoy

Special Teams charts: Ashburn

Practice Organization

 # Practice

Organizing practice is one of the most important aspects of any offense. In this offense it is a little unique since we ask our athletes to perform different skills. This should allow you to master those skills by spending a lot of time on them. Again, I would caution all coaches to master a few skills instead of "dabble" in many.

In this section you will find:

1) Theory behind building a great practice
2) Working Individual Time
3) POD Time – blending your positions
4) Inside/7 on 7
5) Team – Working SITUATIONAL FOOTBALL

Practice

How to structure it in Practice

-Individual time: Coaches working drills against technique we will see in a game. We need to work "all situations" so that is on Wednesday during INDY time. Should be CONSTANT FEEDBACK FROM COACH.

-Group time: Working each run/pass concept vs. predicted front/coverages. On Wednesday we will work "other looks". This time needs to be faster pace, but still take time on feedback.

-Team: Work situations in each rep from the defense. We usually only work predicted front with 5-10 "inserts" each week in team.

All practices need to contain at least 3 elements

-Individual time: Working on specific skills and developing each player.

-Group time: Smaller groups (I will go in detail on how we use "PODS" and Inside/7 on 7 later) to work on timing.

-Team time: This is where each team must practice the situations of the game.

Practice

General Tips for Practice

If needed have your scout defensive coach move players to where the play is going go get a better look.

Always explain "why" during individual. We want to move fast, but not if our players don't get the concepts.

Team work should be working situations against what we predict we will see from a defense.

Don't forget to give 5-10 plays that you allow the Scout DC to "do whatever"

Picking a scout team defensive coordinator needs to become an area of importance. This coach needs to motivate and align many players that may not be very excited to practice.

Individual time does not need to always be "high in tempo". It can be slowed down to make sure everyone understands the goals. The goal is quality of quantity of reps (especially early in the year).

Don't limit your scout team to only the predicted look, be sure to work multiple fronts each week so you are always prepared. Spend 90% of the time on the prediction, but be ready.

Practice

Practicing Structure

Structure your days of the week so that you can get each situation you may face – Here is what we do on offense and defense each day:

Monday – Base plays, adjustments, game plan adjustments, 3rd/4th and shorts, installs

Tuesday – Hash work, Red zone work, 3rd and longs, 2 Minute drill

Wednesday – Short yardage, Gimmicks, Special Formations, 4 Minute drill
*Other defensive looks in individual and pod time (not in team)

Thursday – Review all situations and hit all (time scenarios)

Work to set up a system that you will cover every situation during team time. We use Individual/POD time to cover "series". So we work Buck/Belly/Counter/Jet one day a week inside of individual or POD work.

During team we want to make sure we cover every scenario we may see. Above is how I break down our situations.

 # Film Time

Film Time

Basic layout of film and game plan installation
- Monday: - Game plan goes out (make it unique to each group)
  - Our own film (team 3 good, 3 bad) as a team
  *- Break in groups as much as possible (20-20)

- Tuesday: - Opponent film in groups before practice (pick film)

- Wednesday: Practice film of us in pods/group/team

- Thursday: - Mix of practice film (trouble areas) and game film

As I have progressed as a coach I have seen the enormous benefits of film. Not just to break down and opponent, but to break down our players.

We attempt to get film every day. Early in the week we break down our game from the previous week and the opponent. We film as much as possible on Tuesday and Wednesday and watch that with our athletes on Wednesday/Thursday.

Coaching is great – but showing them on film will get quicker results.

Practice

Practice

In this next section I am going to walk through a variety of my practice plans. Some are from my time at a 4A school with most players going both ways and some will be from my time at a 6A school where players were able to only play one side of the ball. The first one is during a time when I was practicing our Senior and Junior High together to install our offense and defense with the Varsity coaches.

Each period is 5 minutes

Some of the terminology is not the same

I have included our defensive practice because I feel even if a coach is an offensive coordinator it would be good to understand how it works together.

The top of the practice will show each position we are using. Some years we had enough coaches to cover these positions and some years we did not – you will notice that when you see how we "grouped" them to continue to get the drills in.

Practice

This is a practice from early in the season as we were working to install our offense and defense using varsity and junior high coaches together.

You will notice we ran the same drills with our groups and simply rotated senior high on offense and then defense.

In our group period we worked circuits this week. Working our "POD" system on offense and fits for our defense.

We would split for team time at the end of practice. So that it was always varsity kids against varsity kids.

Time	PD	QB	F and B	Y	X and A	OL	DL	ILB	OLB	DB
	1	Senior High Special Teams				Junior High Tackling				
	2									
	3	Senior High Blocking Circuit				Junior High Special Teams				
	4									
	5	BREAK PERIOD								
	6	FTWK	FTWK	W/ OL		Indy	Jh:Off ball	JH: Agilities		JH: FTWK
	7	Tracks	Tracks	W/ OL		Indy	Jh: Stunts	JH: Horse	JH: 3 F's	JH: Ball
	8	Routes	Ball Drill	W/ WR	Routes	Indy	Jh: Read	JH: Keys	JH: Keys	JH: KEYS
	9	JH: FTWK	JH: FTWK	JH: W/ OL		JH: INDY	Off Ball	Agilities		FTWK
	10	JH: Tracks	JH: Tracks	JH: W/ OL		JH: INDY	Stunts	Horseshoe	3 F's	BALL
	11	JH: Routes	JH: Ball Dr	JH: W/ WR	JH: Routes	JH: INDY	Read	Keys	Keys	KEYS
	12	BREAK PERIOD								
	13	GROUP PERIOD: ROTATE DAYS								
	14	JH: Defensive Hip Drill / DL on Sled				SH: Blocking Circuit with OL / Skill working series				
	15	BREAK PERIOD								
	16	GROUP PERIOD: JH:								
	17									
	18	BREAK PERIOD								
	19	JH: OFFENSIVE TEAM				SH: DEFENSIVE TEAM				
	20									
	21									
	22	SH: OFFENSIVE TEAM				JH: DEFENSIVE TEAM				
	23									
	24									

 # Practice

This is a typical early season practice for us at the 4A level. We would often "steal" time for our Line/QB during specialty and special teams.

Period 5 – POD work: Guards are with QB/F. Our "other linemen" are working down blocks. B/X/A working a route or ball drill

Period 7 – POD work: OL-Backs working Counter (AXE) and QB-WR's working a route concept.

Period 16-17 was base offense (we were working hashes)

Period – 18-19 was NASCAR (or up-tempo offense)

PD	QB	F and B	Y	X and A	OL	DL	ILB	OLB	DB
1	Specialty -- Stretching					Gould With Snappers			
2	XP/FG Team				OL-- Pullers on Chute -- Edwards with Down blocks				
3									
4	BREAK								
5	Buck Reads		Ball Drill	Ball Drill	POD Work (G with backs) - ST/C (Cuts)				
6	Rollouts	Rodeo	Wraps	Ball Drills	Rollout blocking		Defense only -- Film		
7	Smokes	Axe Drill	Axe Drill	Smokes	Axe with Backs				
8	Work 3rd and longs -- 8 plays					(AXE is counter)			
9									
10	BREAK								
11						Heel Line	Tackle	Tackle	Tackle
12	Koby and Williams working snaps on own					Read Blocks	Alley / Hip Drill		Ball
13						Pass Rush session -- 3rd and longs			Footwork
14									Route Review
15	BREAK								
16	Base offense								
17									
18	Nascar offense -- Install "gain of 20"								
19									
20	BREAK								
21	TEAM DEFENSE -- Vs. Trips Looks								
22									
23	CONDITIONING								

HUDL with QB's after practice 20 minutes -- 10 of us in practice and 10 of GCT

Practice

This is a template for those coaches that don't have one-way players, but are attempting to get to one-way.

Notice periods 5-6 are for "crossover" players. So those guys that play the majority of the time one side of the ball can get a little bit of time on the other side of the ball.

We also are working in periods 13-14 and 17-18 a time where are two-way players can get some additional time on both sides of the ball.

PD	QB	T	Y/B	X and A	OL	DL	ILB	OLB	DB	
1	SPECIALTY PERIOD --- DC with Non-specialty defensive players --- OL Coach with all linemen not involved									
2	Coach With Kicker, Coach With PAT Group, Coach With Punter/Snapper, Coach With Returnmen									
3	SPECIAL TEAMS GROUP - ROTATE THROUGH MAIN 4 -- Steal time for QB/OL -- Steal time for DL/ILB or DB/OLB									
4										
5										Crossover
6										
7	BREAK					BREAK				
8										Indy/Pod
9										
10										
11										
12	BREAK					BREAK				
13	1's on 1's - 5 minute offense vs. our defense, 5 minute offense working cards									1 on 1s
14										
15	1 on 1's PASS PERIOD					1 on 1's INSIDE PERIOD				
16										
17	BREAK PERIOD					DEFENSIVE PERSONELL GROUPINGS				Defense groupings
18	OFFENSIVE PERSONNELL OR SPECIALS					BREAK PERIOD				Offense groupings
19	Situational Offensive Period (TEAM)					Situational Defensive Period				Vs. Scout group
20										
21										
22	BREAK									
23	CONDITIONING									
24										

Practice

This is a Monday Practice at a 4A school with multiple players going both ways.

Periods 1-2 we are trying to "steal time" again for linemen, QB's and any WR's that do not return kicks.

Periods 3-6: we are working game plan in run game (since most of our OL never play special teams)

Periods 8-9 – Review of opponent on the field and lining up our scout team for the week.

Periods 10-11 – "Specials" and Adjustments for the week

PD	QB	F and B	Y	X and A	OL	DL	ILB	OLB	DB
1	Snaps/QB's		Punters-Snappers		Returners	OL-DOWN BLOCKS		WR-Ball Drills	
2	Snaps/QB's				Returners	OL-DOWN BLOCKS		PUNT BLOCK	
3	Punt Team								
4	KO					OL -- Discuss Personell and alignment			
5	KOR					Koby with OL			
6	PUNT RETURN								
7	BREAK								
8	Offense -- Review of Stuttgart -- 10 minutes								
9									
10	New Install -- (B/Y switch, BOGO-B Special, HVY REV, Simpson Special, Bus Y Special								
11									
12	BREAK								
13	Review of Stuttgart -- 5 Minutes together with DL								
14									
15	DL/ILB INDY					Formation Review with DB/OLB			
16									

 # Practice

This practice is a Monday at a larger school where most of our players did not go both ways and was later in the season.

Periods 1-5: Specialty, but we are not wasting time with players not involved in specialty – they are getting install or fundamental drill time.

Periods 7-8: warm up period for WR's/QB (Ball drill) and is our "buck day" in indy.

Period 9: working roll out passes. OL working roll out and WR's working route combinations.

Periods 11-14: working specific plays or formations

Period 15-16: Introducing a scout team and the opponent on the field.

PD	QB	T	Y/B	X and A	OL	DL	ILB	OLB	DB	
1	SPECIALTY PERIOD --- MCCOY WITH DEFENSIVE --- ENGLISH WITH ALL LINEMEN									
2	Ashburn with Oliver, Weddle with XP group, White with Punters/snappers, Long with Return men, Simpson where needed									
3	SPECIAL TEAMS GROUP - KICKOFF					OL - WORKING BASE		DL - WORKING PINCH			
4	SPECIAL TEAMS GROUP - PUNT TEAM					Block Destruction					
5	SPECIAL TEAMS KOR / XP-FG TEAM					QB - WR's 1 on 1's with DB's					
6	BREAK									
7			Buck Adj		DOWN BLOCKS	Defeat Blocks	Turnover Period		Tackle		OFFENSE FOCUS
8	G's/T's/Q's - Buck/Pan		Pan	Crack Blocks	Hinge/Cut Blocks	Flat Down the line	Fits together from space		FTWK		
9	Bus Routes	T's with OL	Bus Routes -------		Sprite	HEEL LINE	Keys		Run Fits	Ball Drill	DEFENSE FOCUS
10			With OL		Play Review	READ BLOCK	Fits		Blitzes	Fits on run	
11	BREAK PERIOD										
12	Zebra/Zona Period					PASS RUSH	Time Blitzes	Ball to - Attack	Formations		INDY
13	2 Chainz Period			WR's - Work Ball or Blocking		Blitz Package Review		Ball Away - Peak	Main Routes		
14	Flex Period - 8 Plays							Trips alignment and Main Routes			
15	INTRODUCE MARION - BASE PLAYS					TEAM AGAINST MARION					SCHEME
16										

 # Practice

This is a typical mid-late season Tuesday practice for us. Notice at a larger school we are able to accomplish more in less time as this one is only 18 periods. Earlier in the season or when athletes must go both ways, we typically are closer to 24 periods.

Period 6 is our "pod" time: working B/T/WR's together. Zebra was "zone"

Period 7 is also "pod" time: working counter while WR's are working Quick game concepts and "other linemen" are working double team drill.

Periods 8-12: All working concepts as a group. With Period 11 being another "pod" time.

Period 13-14 was inside drill.

Period 16-18 was team. Notice the situations on the left. 3rd down, hash work and red zone.

PD	QB	T	Y/B	X and A	OL	DL	ILB	OLB	DB	
1	Specialty Period -			60 pre-practice						
2				catches						
3	Kickoff Team				OL - DBL TEAMS		QB- White	DEF - Box Fits		
4	XP/FG Team									
5	POPS	POPS	Buck	POPS	DOWN BLOCK	HEEL LINE	Tackling and fits		FTWK	Indy Offense
6	G's/Nick/T's- Buck		B- Zeb Insert	Blocking	BASE BLOCK	BLOCK REC	Blitzes with OLB/ILB		ROUTES	
7	Q/Y/B/T - Counter PERIOD			Quick game	DBL TEAMS	Stunts	Run Fits	Ball To	Tackle/Fit	Indy Defense/Cross Train
8	Zone PERIOD				ZEBRA PERIOD	Block REC	Block Dest	Ball Away	Ball Drills	
9	BREAK PERIOD					BREAK PERIOD				
10	TRADE/SHIFT PERIOD/NEW SETS-FORMATIONS					STEM PD	MUG/BLUFF	Blitzes	Alignment	Pod/Group Work
11	QB/T/QT/QG- Slow Screen		B/X/A - Crack Blocking		ST/Y/SG/C - Cut	PASS RUSH	Key QB (Pass	Routes	Route Recogn	Primary Spot
12	PA PASS PERIOD					Blitzes with ILB's		Trips - (WIDE TRIPS)		
13	7 on 7 - Defensive focus			Trips/DBLS		Inside drill- Offensive Focus				Good on Good
14				Empty						
15	BREAK PERIOD									
16	Team offense					Team Defense				3rd Down
17										Hash Work
18										Red Zone

 # Practice

This practice was a typical Wednesday Practice. It is very similar to Tuesday's practice (of course working other areas of our offense), but notice we are now working new situations during team periods – 3rd and mediums, short yardage/heavy and working red zone again.

Also, the bottom period is where we work on air some situational football. We work a two-minute drill, XP, Onside Kick, Radar (Personnel package) defense and then a "win the game" two-minute drill.

PD	QB	T	Y/B	X and A	OL	DL	ILB	OLB	DB	
1	Specialty Period -			Pre-Practice	OL - Skip Pulls (G's and QT)			Def - Turnover/Fits		
2			Ball Security		OL - Cuts					
3	KOR				OL - HINGE		QB- White	DEF - Box Fits		
4	Kickoff			QB/WR - Quick Game		Defense - Turnover Period				
5	POPS	POPS	Buck	POPS	DOWN	HEEL LINE	KEYS	TACKLING - CIRCLE		INDY - OFFENSE
6	G's/T's/Q - Belly		B- 2nd Level	Now/Bub	BASE	READ BLCK	FITS FROM SPACE	MAVERICK		
7	Bus Passes	With OL	Y/OL	Flood/Snag	SPLITS CHEATS	Fire Off	KEYS/Fits	FORCE-FIT	ALIGN	INDY - DEFENSE
8	Counter Period - Y/G/T/B/Q			Crack Blocks	Cut/Hinge	DOWN LINE	Off Blocks	Off Blocks	ROUTES	
9	BREAK PERIOD					BREAK PERIOD				
10	FLEX PERIOD					STEMS	RUN FITS	Alignment and Route Recognitio		Pod/Group Work
11	MUSTANG PERIOD					Pass Rush	Drops-Key QB	Fits in run game		Primary Spot
12	PLAY ACTION / SCREEN PERIOD					BLITZ PERIOD FRONT 7			MAVERICK	
13	7 on 7 Period - Priority Defense			Trips/DBLS		Inside Run Period - Offense Priority (English)				
14				Empty						
15	BREAK PERIOD									
16	Team Offense 5 3rd and med, Spread Personnel, RED ZONE					Team Defense - Base, 2 PT Plays, Wildcat				Short Yardage
17										Specials / Heavy
18										Run Game
19	Play the game Situations on Air - 2 minute drive offense - finish with "fire" XP/FG, Onside Kick, RADAR DEFNSE, 2 min drive offense									
20										Short Yardage

67

 # Practice

This is our Thursday practice script. We will modify as needed. But at a larger school we will split the team for the first 15 minutes and review our script, 3rd down plays and usually and "troubled" areas during the week here.

The rest of it is a normal Thursday "Play the game" to review multiple situations.

Play the game

1) Offense (Scripted plays) / 3rd downs - Defense (Base alignment) - Play rev
2) KOR - Middle and Wall
3) Nascar Drive - 6 plays - New grouping each play
4) Punt - Offensive Punt, Base Punt Team
5) Defense - Base Defense
6) Punt Return / Block - Line up
7) 2 min drill - run heavy to score near red zone
8) XP/FG - FREEZE, FIRE
9) Kickoff
10) Radar Defense
11) XP/FG Block
12) KO -- Onside Kicks
13) HANDS TEAM
14) Offense - Review 4 minute (stay in bounds, ball security)
15) Victory formation

Practice: Periods

Individual Drills

Individual

The goal is to work "daily" drills that translate directly to Friday Night
- We want to prioritize the different areas for each position
- Spend the most time on areas that we use the most

We don't want "mindless reps" here, but we do want a high volume of reps

A coach should never "be done" with these drills as they are the foundation to what we do

Build a DRILL BOOK

Individual time should be "sacred" time for all position coaches. This is the time to address specific areas this position group struggled with or to work to highlight skill sets.

Generally, we will give 20-25 minutes a day here early in the season and cut it back to 10-15 minutes as the season progresses, but we are always looking for ways to "steal" time for these players.

Make a priority list on Sunday meetings for the week and then work those priorities in the form of drills throughout the week.

Individual Time

Example – Our "B" (wingback)

Skills needed per position
- Blocking
    - Down blocks
    - Blocking in space
    - Double teams
- Ball drill
    - Ball security
    - Vision
- Catching
    - Chute routes/bubble screens
    - Peak
    - Deeper Routes

This is specific to our "B" in our offense. We want to make sure we hit each of these skills throughout the off-season/pre-season. As the season hits we may cherry-pick areas that need to be addressed.

The goal is to do this with each position. We want to decide what is most important with each player – and then tailor our individual time to work on that role he has in our offense.

Individual Time

Example – Our "B" (wingback)
- Blocking (25 minutes a week in individual, 20 minutes in "pods")
    - Down blocks – Main block needed (prioritize) – 20 Indy, 5 Pod
    - Blocking in space – Second block needed – 5 Indy, 10 in Pod
    - Double teams – Needs to work with TE – 5 in Pod
- Ball drill (10 minutes a week in individual, 10 minutes in "pods")
    - Ball security
    - Vision
- Catching (5 minutes a week in individual, 10 minutes in "pods")
    - Chute routes/bubble screens
    - Peak
    - Deeper Routes

*Use "POD" time to teach skills another coach is more comfortable teaching

This is how we design how much time (early in season) we will dedicate to drills for our "B". We look at the skill areas needed to be addressed and then prioritize them.

We then decide which type of drill he needs.

Working backwards to fill in the practice schedule to match the skills needed is much easier after you have prioritized what is needed.

Individual Time

Using Individual and Adjustments

Offensive line – Working the technique over the alignment (it changes often for us)
- Monday/Tuesday/Thursday – Predicted front/technique
- Wednesday – Other front/techniques/Blitzes to be prepared

WR – Set Indy time for what we expect
- Release Drill
- Screen concepts vs. off/press coverage
- Route adjustments
- *Always work man-press on Wednesday to be prepared

This is how we structure our offensive line and WR time during the season. We want to make sure we are working expected fronts/coverages for 3 of the 4 days that week and then working a "worst case scenario".

This needs to be done in individual time as we may not have much time during team/inside drill to hit multiple looks.

 # Individual

Using Individual and Adjustments

QB – We predict fronts and coverages, but work all RPO/Pass Concepts

-Make it hard on him Tuesday, but he needs to play/feel "clean" on Wednesday/Thursday (confidence is king)

-Work new adjustments in Indy/Pod time and on air to make sure he is ready before doing it in "Team"

-Individual and Pod time is as important as team, so be sure to rep all the potential reads during his normal "drills"

This is how we structure our QB's week. We want Monday to be a "game plan" day. Tuesday it may look ugly as we throw a lot at him. We want to see what he can handle and what we feel good about heading into Wednesday.

Wednesday should look much cleaner as we have streamlined the game plan for him. Thursday should almost be boring for him.

 # "Pod" work

PODS

This is to work areas of our offense that need to work together
- Guards and Skill players on run game
- WR's and QT on screen game
- QB and OL – on runs/blitz pickup
- Wingback/TE with OL Coach
- Wingback with WR Coach

*The goal here is to put coach with expertise coaching the skill --

This is the area we separate our system from most others. I believe the POD system we have started is one of the best things we do in practice. This allows us to maximize time, reps and handle more players with less coaches.

It also allows coaches to work with different players which leads to better team cohesion.

In the next pages I will go through a few different set ups we use.

 # "Pod" work

This is the first type of POD we use when we are working Buck Sweep.

Guards and QB/RB together in the middle.

OL – Working down blocks in left corner

Y/B – Working scenarios on down block in right corner

WR's – Working screen/quick game/blocking at bottom

5 minute period with a lot of reps. We will change up the QB read each time.

 # "Pod" work

This is a close-up of our POD drill time for buck sweep. Notice we have a line coach, RB coach and QB coach all involved in this POD. At this school I was blessed to have multiple coaches working the offensive side of the ball.

At other schools, this POD has been run by one coach due to not having as many coaches available.

 # "Pod" work

This POD is our "Belly" POD.

We are working guards on wrap blocking with QB/RB.

At the bottom we have our WR/B working blocking in space for screens.

At the top right we have our other linemen working double teams.

 # "Pod" work

This POD is our slow screen POD.

We are working slow screens with our QT/QG and RB/QB.

At the top our other linemen are working pass pro.

At the bottom you can see our WR/B working crack blocking.

 # Inside-RPO

The next section of our practice is our "Inside" period. During this time we often will pair up a quick game period.

For instance, all the line, B, F and QB will be working run game. On the other end of the field our X/A (and sometimes B) will be working screen/quick game.

This period is generally on Tuesday/Wednesday for 10 minutes and we want to be sure to hit all our base runs. We want high tempo and to record this period.

Here is an example of 2019. Right off the picture to the left is our WR coach working with our X/A. The rest of our offense is working inside drill and our "steal" RPO for the QB.

# Team

In my opinion this is the area of practices most coaches begin to lose their athletes. If done correctly, each athlete has already worked on the skills and this time should be a "game-like" scenario.

To help this happen I script situations for every snap during team. From hash work to 3rd downs to red zone to time management. We want to cover all of these as we are getting "reps" with our plays.

Early in the season I'd recommend doing this by "series". Or working buck series, belly series, etc… As you get closer to the season and during in-season practices it is always best to work plays as you'd call them in a game. So working "situational football" is the best way to run your team sessions of practice.

On the next page I go through how I have chosen to break it down. This will insure as a coach you (AND YOUR PLAYERS) understand what plays you plan to call for every situation. Knowing as a coach is great, but having your team know and feel confident is the key.

Team

16	Team offense	Team Defense	3rd Down
17			Hash Work
18			Red Zone

16	Team Offense 5 3rd and med, Spread Personnel, RED ZONE	Team Defense - Base, 2 PT Plays, Wildcat	Short Yardage
17			Specials / Heavy
18			Run Game
19	Play the game Situations on Air - 2 minute drive offense - finish with "fire" XP/FG, Onside Kick, RADAR DEFNSE, 2 min drive offense		
20			Short Yardage

Here are a few examples of how we do "team" above.

Remember to organize each day to hit all situations you will face in a game. Below are what I'd recommend.

Practicing Structure

Structure your days of the week so that you can get each situation you may face – Here is what we do on offense and defense each day:

Monday – Base plays, adjustments, game plan adjustments, 3rd/4th and shorts, installs

Tuesday – Hash work, Red zone work, 3rd and longs, 2 Minute drill

Wednesday – Short yardage, Gimmicks, Special Formations, 4 Minute drill
*Other defensive looks in individual and pod time (not in team)

Thursday – Review all situations and hit all (time scenarios)

Adding "wrinkles"

 # Formations

Formations are an area that can be complicated in any offense or sometimes overly simple. Each year I explore a few formations that may give our team an advantage, but I live by the rule – simple is best. If a team runs too many formations, it can be difficult to predict how a defense will react and thus difficult to teach your athletes what to expect. On the flip side, if an offense lives in 1-2 formations the majority of the game, the defense may be able to create multiple looks to attack it with no fear of an answer.

In this section, I will share a variety of looks this offense can get into with one or two word tags. I'd caution you as a coach to be sure you are great at your base before working these additional formations. Generally if we are using multiple formations we are doing so for one of the following reasons:

1) Exploit a weakness we have seen in defensive alignment
2) Attack a player on the defense by getting him isolated
3) Matching personnel with better formations – you may have a player that is better in space or not as good in space
4) Move away from stronger players on defense – get the defense to put best players one place and then go the other direction.

 # Formations

Under each formation, I will list a few concepts we use. Again, I want to caution that if you become "formation dependent" (or only run certain plays from certain formations) you will become easier to defend. The goal is to run as many of your base concepts from any formation that is used.

While we do more things from these formations I am going to list and show, it will give you a good idea of how to take these formations and work towards creating matchups that will benefit your offense.

In each section you will find –
Base sets and easy tags that fit with base formations

Remember, in this offense, each play is able to be run from each formation, as long as the defense gives the look that is desired.

*There are more formations available in the other Gun T books, these are just meant to be the base ones I begin with.

Power of Formations

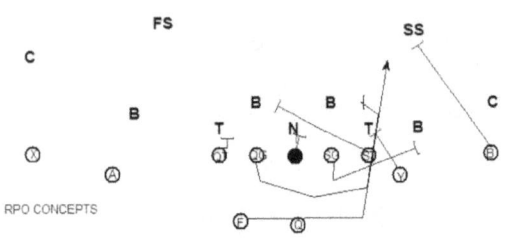

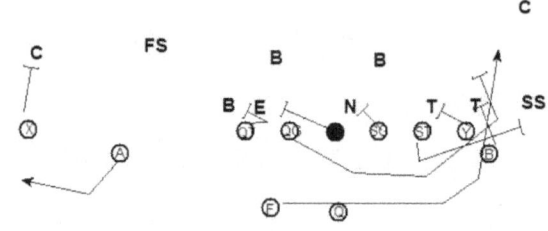

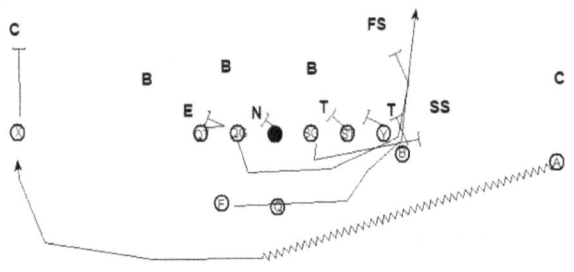

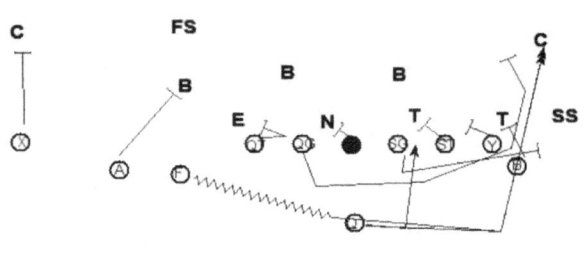

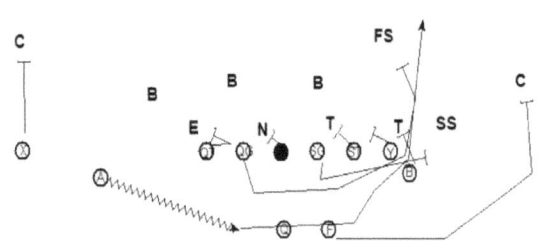

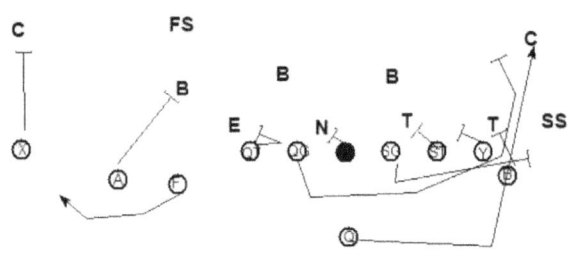

This is Buck Sweep run from multiple formations and from multiple motions. I use this as simply and example of why formations and motions matter in this offense. Running the base play is most important, but being able to motion and use formation gives a great advantage.

Formations on left side of column:
Pro
Flop – Train Motion
Strong – Train Motion

Right side column:
Red
Empty – Fly Motion
Empty

 # Red

Position	Alignment
X	Top of the numbers
A	Split X and QT off the ball
F	Heels on QB toes. Split the QG and QT
Y	Head even with hip of center. 2 ft splits
B	2x2 off Y
QT	Head even with hip of center. 2 ft splits
QG	Head even with hip of center. 2 ft splits
C	On Ball
SG	Head even with hip of center. 2 ft splits
ST	Head even with hip of center. 2 ft splits
Q	Heels at 5 yards

Blue

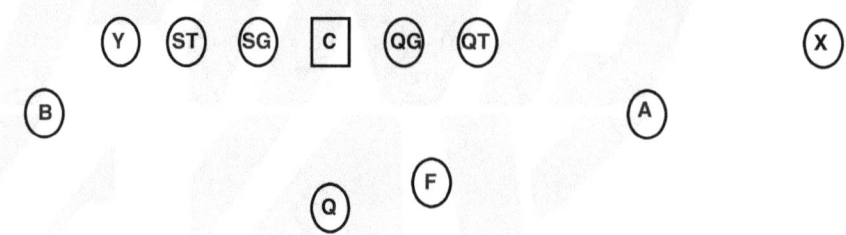

Position	Alignment
X	Top of the numbers
A	Split X and QT off the ball
F	Heels on QB toes. Split the QG and QT
Y	Head even with hip of center. 2 ft splits
B	2x2 off Y
QT	Head even with hip of center. 2 ft splits
QG	Head even with hip of center. 2 ft splits
C	On Ball
SG	Head even with hip of center. 2 ft splits
ST	Head even with hip of center. 2 ft splits
Q	Heels at 5 yards

Red
Flop

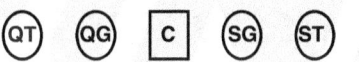

Position	Alignment
X	Top of the numbers
A	On numbers to the strong side
F	Heels on QB toes. Split the QG and QT
Y	Head even with hip of center. 2 ft splits
B	2x2 off Y
QT	Head even with hip of center. 2 ft splits
QG	Head even with hip of center. 2 ft splits
C	On Ball
SG	Head even with hip of center. 2 ft splits
ST	Head even with hip of center. 2 ft splits
Q	Heels at 5 yards

Blue
Flop

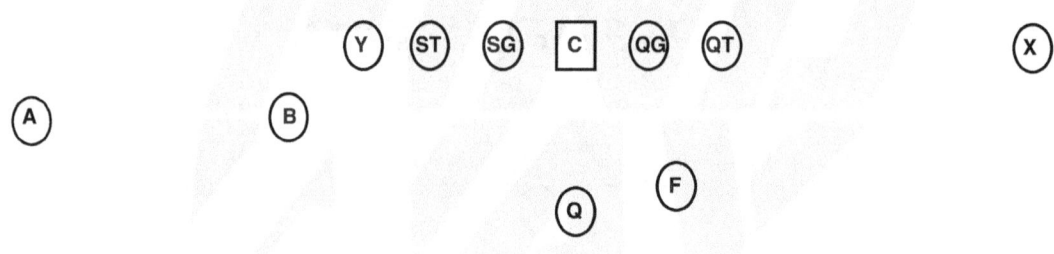

Position	Alignment
X	Top of the numbers
A	On numbers to strong side
F	Heels on QB toes. Split the QG and QT
Y	Head even with hip of center. 2 ft splits
B	2x2 off Y
QT	Head even with hip of center. 2 ft splits
QG	Head even with hip of center. 2 ft splits
C	On Ball
SG	Head even with hip of center. 2 ft splits
ST	Head even with hip of center. 2 ft splits
Q	Heels at 5 yards

Red
Empty

X　　　　　　　　QT QG C SG ST Y
　　A　　F　　　　　　　　　　　B

　　　　　　　　　Q

Position	Alignment
X	Top of the numbers
A	Split X and QT off the ball
F	Split A and QT off the ball
Y	Head even with hip of center. 2 ft splits
B	2x2 off Y
QT	Head even with hip of center. 2 ft splits
QG	Head even with hip of center. 2 ft splits
C	On Ball
SG	Head even with hip of center. 2 ft splits
ST	Head even with hip of center. 2 ft splits
Q	Heels at 5 yards

Blue
Empty

Position	Alignment
X	Top of the numbers
A	Split X and QT off the ball
F	Split A and QT off the ball
Y	Head even with hip of center. 2 ft splits
B	2x2 off Y
QT	Head even with hip of center. 2 ft splits
QG	Head even with hip of center. 2 ft splits
C	On Ball
SG	Head even with hip of center. 2 ft splits
ST	Head even with hip of center. 2 ft splits
Q	Heels at 5 yards

Red
Lion

Position	Alignment
X	Top of the numbers
A	Split X and QT off the ball
F	Heels on QB toes. Split the QG and QT
Y	Head even with hip of center. 2 ft splits
B	Split A and QT off the ball
QT	Head even with hip of center. 2 ft splits
QG	Head even with hip of center. 2 ft splits
C	On Ball
SG	Head even with hip of center. 2 ft splits
ST	Head even with hip of center. 2 ft splits
Q	Heels at 5 yards

17

Blue
Roar

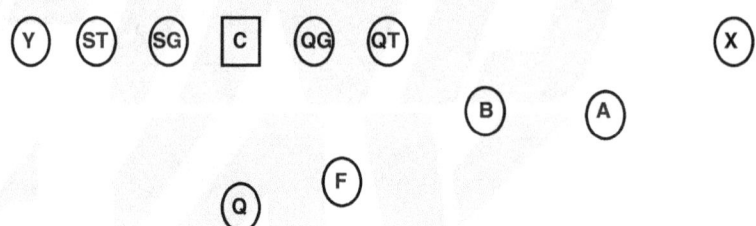

Position	Alignment
X	Top of the numbers
A	Split X and QT off the ball
F	Heels on QB toes. Split the QG and QT
Y	Head even with hip of center. 2 ft splits
B	Split A and QT off the ball
QT	Head even with hip of center. 2 ft splits
QG	Head even with hip of center. 2 ft splits
C	On Ball
SG	Head even with hip of center. 2 ft splits
ST	Head even with hip of center. 2 ft splits
Q	Heels at 5 yards

Red
Strong

Position	Alignment
X	Top of the numbers
A	Split X and QT off the ball
F	Heels on QB toes. Split the SG and ST
Y	Head even with hip of center. 2 ft splits
B	2x2 off Y
QT	Head even with hip of center. 2 ft splits
QG	Head even with hip of center. 2 ft splits
C	On Ball
SG	Head even with hip of center. 2 ft splits
ST	Head even with hip of center. 2 ft splits
Q	Heels at 5 yards

Blue
Strong

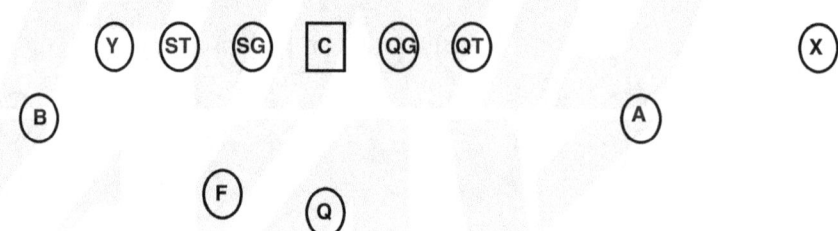

Position	Alignment
X	Top of the numbers
A	Split X and QT off the ball
F	Heels on QB toes. Split the SG and ST
Y	Head even with hip of center. 2 ft splits
B	2x2 off Y
QT	Head even with hip of center. 2 ft splits
QG	Head even with hip of center. 2 ft splits
C	On Ball
SG	Head even with hip of center. 2 ft splits
ST	Head even with hip of center. 2 ft splits
Q	Heels at 5 yards

Red
Squeeze

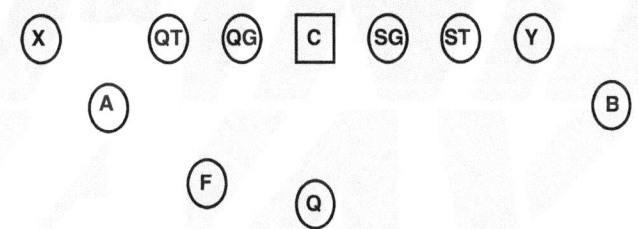

Position	Alignment
X	2 yards outside A on line of scrimmage
A	2x2 off QT
F	Heels on QB toes. Split the QG and QT
Y	Head even with hip of center. 2 ft splits
B	2x2 off Y
QT	Head even with hip of center. 2 ft splits
QG	Head even with hip of center. 2 ft splits
C	On Ball
SG	Head even with hip of center. 2 ft splits
ST	Head even with hip of center. 2 ft splits
Q	Heels at 5 yards

Blue
Squeeze

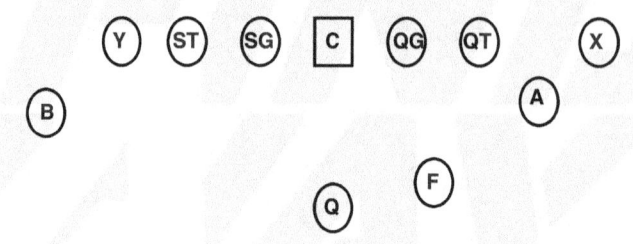

Position	Alignment
X	2 yards outside A on line of scrimmage
A	2x2 off QT
F	Heels on QB toes. Split the QG and QT
Y	Head even with hip of center. 2 ft splits
B	2x2 off Y
QT	Head even with hip of center. 2 ft splits
QG	Head even with hip of center. 2 ft splits
C	On Ball
SG	Head even with hip of center. 2 ft splits
ST	Head even with hip of center. 2 ft splits
Q	Heels at 5 yards

Red
Empty Squeeze

Position	Alignment
X	2 yards outside A on the line of scrimmage
A	2 yards outside F off the ball
F	2x2 off QT
Y	Head even with hip of center. 2 ft splits
B	2x2 off Y
QT	Head even with hip of center. 2 ft splits
QG	Head even with hip of center. 2 ft splits
C	On Ball
SG	Head even with hip of center. 2 ft splits
ST	Head even with hip of center. 2 ft splits
Q	Heels at 5 yards

Blue
Empty Squeeze

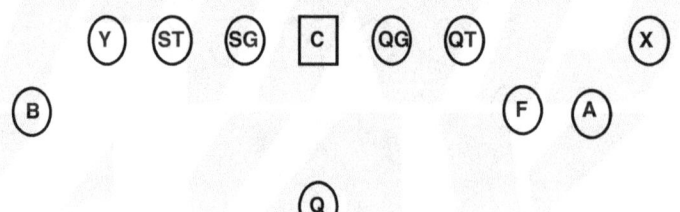

Position	Alignment
X	2 yards outside A on line of scrimmage
A	2 yards outside F off the ball
F	2x2 off QT
Y	Head even with hip of center. 2 ft splits
B	2x2 off Y
QT	Head even with hip of center. 2 ft splits
QG	Head even with hip of center. 2 ft splits
C	On Ball
SG	Head even with hip of center. 2 ft splits
ST	Head even with hip of center. 2 ft splits
Q	Heels at 5 yards

Red
Lion Squeeze

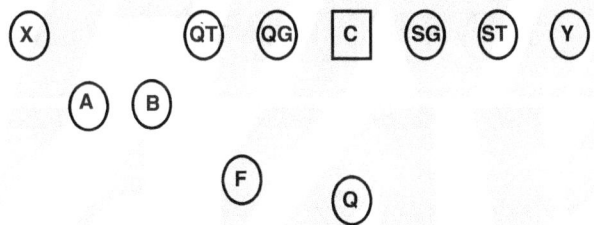

Position	Alignment
X	2 yards outside A on line of scrimmage
A	2 yards outside B on line of scrimmage
F	Heels on QB toes. Split the QG and QT
Y	Head even with hip of center. 2 ft splits
B	2x2 off QT
QT	Head even with hip of center. 2 ft splits
QG	Head even with hip of center. 2 ft splits
C	On Ball
SG	Head even with hip of center. 2 ft splits
ST	Head even with hip of center. 2 ft splits
Q	Heels at 5 yards

Blue
Roar

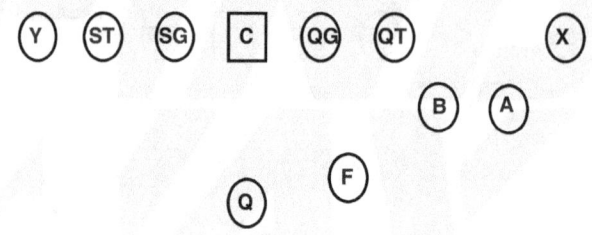

Position	Alignment
X	2 yards outside A on line of scrimmage
A	2 yards outside B off the ball
F	Heels on QB toes. Split the QG and QT
Y	Head even with hip of center. 2 ft splits
B	2x2 off QT
QT	Head even with hip of center. 2 ft splits
QG	Head even with hip of center. 2 ft splits
C	On Ball
SG	Head even with hip of center. 2 ft splits
ST	Head even with hip of center. 2 ft splits
Q	Heels at 5 yards

Red
Flex

Position	Alignment
X	Top of the numbers
A	Split X and QT off the ball
F	Heels on QB toes. Split the QG and QT
Y	6 yards outside of B on line of scrimmage
B	2x2 off ST
QT	Head even with hip of center. 2 ft splits
QG	Head even with hip of center. 2 ft splits
C	On Ball
SG	Head even with hip of center. 2 ft splits
ST	Head even with hip of center. 2 ft splits
Q	Heels at 5 yards

Blue
Flex

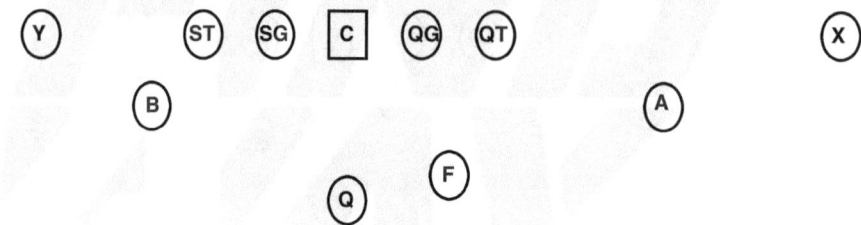

Position	Alignment
X	Top of the numbers
A	Split X and QT off the ball
F	Heels on QB toes. Split the QG and QT
Y	6 yards outside of B on line of scrimmage
B	2x2 off ST
QT	Head even with hip of center. 2 ft splits
QG	Head even with hip of center. 2 ft splits
C	On Ball
SG	Head even with hip of center. 2 ft splits
ST	Head even with hip of center. 2 ft splits
Q	Heels at 5 yards

Red
Empty Flop

Position	Alignment
X	Top of the numbers
A	On numbers to the strong side
F	Split QT and X off the ball
Y	Head even with hip of center. 2 ft splits
B	2x2 off Y
QT	Head even with hip of center. 2 ft splits
QG	Head even with hip of center. 2 ft splits
C	On Ball
SG	Head even with hip of center. 2 ft splits
ST	Head even with hip of center. 2 ft splits
Q	Heels at 5 yards

Blue
Empty Flop

Position	Alignment
X	Top of the numbers
A	On numbers to strong side
F	Split QT and X off the ball
Y	Head even with hip of center. 2 ft splits
B	2x2 off Y
QT	Head even with hip of center. 2 ft splits
QG	Head even with hip of center. 2 ft splits
C	On Ball
SG	Head even with hip of center. 2 ft splits
ST	Head even with hip of center. 2 ft splits
Q	Heels at 5 yards

Red
Empty Lion

Position	Alignment
X	Top of the numbers
A	Split X and QT off the ball
F	Split QT and B off the ball
Y	Head even with hip of center. 2 ft splits
B	Split A and F off the ball
QT	Head even with hip of center. 2 ft splits
QG	Head even with hip of center. 2 ft splits
C	On Ball
SG	Head even with hip of center. 2 ft splits
ST	Head even with hip of center. 2 ft splits
Q	Heels at 5 yards

Blue
Empty Roar

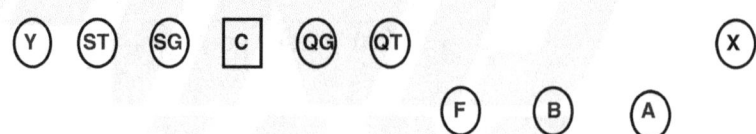

Position	Alignment
X	Top of the numbers
A	Split X and B off the ball
F	Split B and QT off the ball
Y	Head even with hip of center. 2 ft splits
B	Split A and F off the ball
QT	Head even with hip of center. 2 ft splits
QG	Head even with hip of center. 2 ft splits
C	On Ball
SG	Head even with hip of center. 2 ft splits
ST	Head even with hip of center. 2 ft splits
Q	Heels at 5 yards

 # Formations

My goal with formations has been pretty simple – If I feel that a formation can give me an advantage, then we want to be able to line up in that formation. This offense is built to have simple tags to give multiple looks to a defense. As the coach and the QB there is much to learn, but to position players it is very simple.

Timeline:

Off-season/Spring
-Work a formation period each session for 5 minutes
-Work motions and shifts (pick 1) for 5 minutes

Summer/Early Season
-Work a formation period in skill sections each day
-Work motions and shifts (pick 1) each day for 5 minutes

In-season
-Review formations on Monday
-Work all shifts in group/team work

Game-Plan
-While we can run any formation if needed, we generally pick 4-5 formations and 1 trade/shift we like each week depending on the match-up.

Shifts-Cheats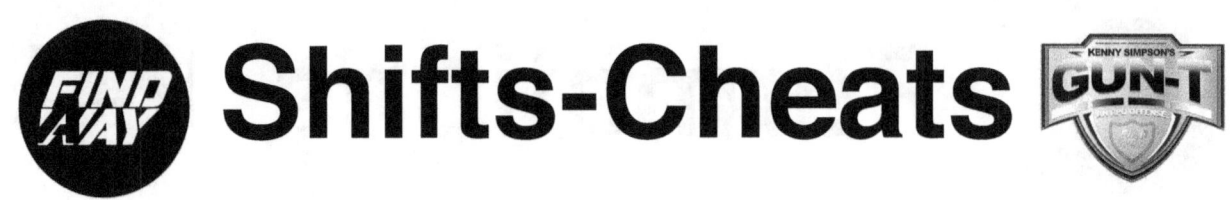

Using motions and shifts has become something many offenses are starting to use. I highly recommend using them to "spice" up or give your offense an advantage. Here are a few simple ones:

1) Linemen splits – Teach your line to cheat splits on Belly or any gap play to create larger natural gaps. Also, teach them to cheat closer for double teams. This may sound basic, but it has really helped our offensive line.

2) Use motion more often against man-to-man teams. Those teams will kill your RPO game, but you can make up for it by shifting and quick motioning.

3) Quick huddle – I don't talk a lot about quick huddling, but if you want to gain an advantage huddling 2 yards off the ball with your line and then getting on the ball and snapping it quickly will make it difficult for the defense to adapt.

4) Using "over" sets where your tight end lines up weak will also cause issues with a defense identifying strength if you do them quickly and can create and uncovered player.

Opponent Prep

My goal when scouting opponents is to ensure that we focus mostly on the ability level of the opponent. With this offense we will see multiple looks that are not the same as they would show against a "10 personnel" team or "normal offense". So while we do work predicted alignment, we are more concerned with the following:

1) Studs and Duds – in the box and in the secondary
2) Technique of the DL/ILB – Squeeze and pinch or up-field disrupters
3) Keys oriented or blitz/movement oriented

We will also look over as much film as possible to see what their potential adjustments are to a TE/Wing look. Often you may see similar looks and be able to make an educated guess as to what the defense will do.

Opponent Prep

Scouting Opponents for Offense

What to do with your game plan based on opponents
- Coverage checks and Passing game tweaks
- When is the best time to take a shot on offense – and at who?
- When do they go "goal line"
- Who to attack and who to avoid?
- What will they key on your offense – can you do false keys/tendency breakers?

*This is our Coaching checklist

This is my checklist for scouting an opponent each week. I usually will delegate parts of this out to my assistant coaches so that we can focus on a few of these areas.

One coach for us always handles back-end of the defense, while another (OL coach) looks at the front.

Usually I work on the field areas, tendency breakers and false keys.

Opponent Prep

Scouting Opponents for Offense

Offensive line – Are they pressure team or technique? Any tells in stance to blitzes or stunts?

QB – Coverages and guys to avoid? Who is aggressive/passive in coverage? Do we think LB/DL will take the give or QB?

WR – Coverages and technique of DB's?

TE/Wings – Same concepts as the offensive line and WR's

This is what we want our athletes to know. I want my coaches to know much more about our opponent, but we want to be very careful with how much we give our athletes.

This list is the minimum I want my athletes to know. If they can handle more information we want them to have it.

Example – A senior QB we will give much more of the game plan to than a sophomore RB.

Creating A Call Sheet

Creating A Call Sheet

Goals for play calling are to be as efficient as possible. In the excitement of the game, often times we will forget concepts we wanted to use to take advantage of the defense. So the goal of a call sheet is to be of assistance.

Here are my goals:

Gaining Knowledge Early – I want to confirm what I have seen on film all week. To do this I will have an opening script that works multiple formations, shifts and false-keys.

Take pressure off big downs – Nothing is more stressful as a coach than those 3rd/4th down calls. Working this throughout the week and putting it on a call sheet helps to give at least a smaller "menu" of plays to call.

Plays for your best athletes – Football is won and lost by players. Our job is to make sure we are giving them every advantage. On my sheet I have an entire section of plays to make sure these guys touch the ball.

Include a time chart and a 2-point chart – Time and score management are critical and math skills under pressure are not always a great skill set of many coaches. Work this chart so when those moments come you are ready.

 # Creating A Call Sheet

Drive Starters		2 MINUTE		Palmer	F	Play Script		
Trips: Sword/B Peak	25	Fish	2	Cannon	Cannon	Flop-Train - Cannon/Bubble	4	Palmer
Arrow-Jokers	33	Trips/Quads-42 Fas	24	Sword	Sword	RBBT GROUP - Bus Arrow JOKE	33	Duncan
Bulldog/Quads Runs		Jail/A Jail		F - Draw	F Draw	Trips - Run/Screen		Palmer/Haas
Bus Arrow	1	Laser	21	Cnn THBCK	F Wheel	R/B - Sword/Fast	11	Palmer
Cannon-Steal/Key	1	A Throwback	31	TRAP	Empty Screens	Bulldog - Cannon	1	Larkin
Flop-Cannon	32	RAIL (TRIPS)	52	F KNIFE	Jail-JET	R/B - Q KNIFE	2	Jones
2nd and SHOTS		**Screen Game**		Empty - 43	B-Arrow	Bus-Arrow	1	Larkin
Simpson Special	13	42 Fast	24	Jail - Swing	B- Axe	QUADS - 42 Fast	24	Haas
Jail and Go	34	Jail/A Jail		Boise - Swing	A - Train Jet/Cnn	Flop - Cannon	32	Fraiser
Jet Pass	15	Laser		LASER		RBBT GROUP - BUS KNIFE	2	Jones
3rd and longs		Empty 43	2	**"A"**	**"A"**	**Plays to run 1st Half**		
Jail/A Jail		Axe Shuffle		Jail and Go	Fish/Snag	Simpson Special	13	Shane/Fraiser
BEAR ROLL	22	**RED ZONE**		A Throwback	Train Runs	Flop - CN CRACK AND GO		Dugger
		Bus-Arrow	35	Peak	Peak - Base			
Trips-Fish	2	CNN STAY	43	**"B"**	**"X"**	**Plays for 2nd half**		
Laser -- Fraiser	21	POWER	45	Axe/Arrow	Snag - Snag Switch	Jail and Go	34	Dugger/Haas
3rd and Shorts		Q RUNS		Shark/Bear	Jail	BOGO	42	Shane
Arrow	1	HEAVY		B GO	Water-Pyramid	B SPECIAL	45	Larkin
CNN STAY	51	Bus - A THOWBCK	31	**Shane**	**HAAS PLAYS**	BUS - STRIKER	24	Shane
POWER	45	**2 Point Plays**		Fast/Jail	A-JET			
Q RUNS - HEAVY		FIRE on XP/FG		X Slugo	QB - Knife	**NOTES FOR PLAYS-FORMATIONS**		
3rd and Mediums		Bus-Rub	3	Snag	QB - Sword/Cannon	Flop - DO WE LIGHTEN THE BOX -- TRAIN??		
Bus Arrow Joker	33	Heavy	1	Pyramid	QB - Rollouts	BULLDOG -- Can we run to the Trips		
Trips/Quads 42 Fast	31	**SHOT PLAYS**		**Landan at QB**	A - Jail	JOKER-- KEYING GUARDS --		
Sword	11	Jail and Go	34	Base Runs	A - Peak	3rd Down ILB's love to blitz -- Arrow/CNN Stay/PW		
CNN STAY	43	Crack and Go		Bus - Pass Routes - Q Arrow		BOGO/JAIL AND GO -- Set up and throw TD's		
4th and shorts		Empty Flex Nasty		Q runs-Cannon/Sword/G	**FALSE KEYS**	RBBT Group -- Arrow and see how they handl mot		
Arrow (Larkin)	1			Fast/Jail	GUT	QB keeping off "Steal" and "Key" will be big		
CNN STAY	43	Axe Y Special			ARROW Joker	Ride what got us here -- but be ready to adjust		
Q Runs (KNIFE)	2	Train-DBL Pass			BAM			
4th and longs					**SHOTS/GIMMICKS**	**Timeouts**		
A Throwback	31				Simpson Special	If they have 0 Time-outs		2:00
FISH	2	**Play after turnover**		**HEAVY PLAYS**	Jet Pass	If they have 1 Time-out		1:25
SNAG	1	Train-DBL Pass		Power	Jail and Go's	If they have 2 Time-outs		0:50
MAN ZERO CALLS		X Reverse Pass		Axe	X Reverse Pass	If they have 3 Time-outs		0:20
Bus Routes - Throwback		**Backed UP**		Cannon		**PAT CHART**		
Jail		Q RUNS		Cannon-Pass		Go for 2 if...		
Jail and Go		Sword		Simpson Special		Ahead: 1,4,5,11,12,19		
Bear						Behind: 2,5,10,16,17,18,21,25		

Creating A Call Sheet

Drive Starters		2 MINUTE	
Trips: Sword/B Peak	25	Fish	2
Arrow-Jokers	33	Trips/Quads-42 Fast	24
Bulldog/Quads Runs		Jail/A Jail	
Bus Arrow	1	Laser	21
Cannon-Steal/Key	1	A Throwback	31
Flop-Cannon	32	RAIL (TRIPS)	52
2nd and SHOTS		Screen Game	
Simpson Special	13	42 Fast	24
Jail and Go	34	Jail/A Jail	
Jet Pass	15	Laser	
3rd and longs		Empty 43	2
Jail/A Jail		Axe Shuffle	32
BEAR ROLL	22	RED ZONE	
		Bus-Arrow	35
Trips-Fish	2	CNN STAY	43
Laser -- Fraiser	21	POWER	45
3rd and Shorts		Q RUNS	
Arrow	1	HEAVY	
CNN STAY	51	Bus - A THOWBCK	31
POWER	45	2 Point Plays	
Q RUNS - HEAVY		FIRE on XP/FG	
3rd and Mediums		Bus-Rub	3
Bus-Arrow Joker	33	Heavy	1
Trips/Quads 42 Fast	31	SHOT PLAYS	
Sword	11	Jail and Go	34
CNN STAY	43	Crack and Go	
4th and shorts		Empty Flex - Nasty	
Arrow (Larkin)	1		
CNN STAY	43	Axe Y Special	
Q Runs (KNIFE)	2	Train-DBL Pass	
4th and longs			
A Throwback	31		
FISH	2	Play after turnover	
SNAG	1	Train-DBL Pass	
MAN ZERO CALLS		X Reverse Pass	
Bus Routes - Throwback		Backed UP	
Jail		Q RUNS	
Jail and Go		Sword	
Bear			

This is the left column of my play sheet.

"Drive Starters" are plays for if we are struggling on first down.

The rest of the left column is plays for situations.

I always want the bottom to include a "man-zero" game plan and a "backed-up" series.

The next part is more situational football –

2 minute plays we like.
Screens
Red Zone Plays
2 Point Plays

Shot plays for us are any potentially explosive plays or "specials"

As you can see we change our verbiage each season. On this sheet:

Sword – Belly
Arrow – Jet
Cannon – Buck
Fish - Flood

Creating A Call Sheet

Palmer		F	
Cannon		Cannon	
Sword		Sword	
F - Draw		F Draw	
Cnn THBCK		F Wheel	
TRAP		Empty Screens	
F KNIFE		Jail-JET	
Empty - 43		B-Arrow	
Jail - Swing		B- Axe	
Boise - Swing		A - Train Jet/Cnn	
LASER			
"A"		"A"	
Jail and Go		Fish/Snag	
A Throwback		Train Runs	
Peak		Peak - Base	
"B"		"X"	
Axe/Arrow		Snag - Snag Switch	
Shark/Bear		Jail	
B GO		Water-Pyramid	
Shane		HAAS PLAYS	
Fast/Jail		A-JET	
X Slugo		QB - Knife	
Snag		QB - Sword/Cannon	
Pyramid		QB - Rollouts	
Landan at QB		A - Jail	
Base Runs		A - Peak	
Bus - Pass Routes - Q Arrow			
Q runs-Cannon/Sword/G		FALSE KEYS	
Fast/Jail		GUT	
		ARROW Joker	
		BAM	
		SHOTS/GIMMICKS	
		Simpson Special	
HEAVY PLAYS		Jet Pass	
Power		Jail and Go's	
Axe		X Reverse Pass	
Cannon			
Cannon-Pass			
Simpson Special			

The next part of our call sheet is plays for Players.

I usually will dedicate a section to which player I feel is our best player that year. In this example that was "Palmer" and "Haas"

We also try to include plays that go to certain positions. This makes it easy to get the ball to a guy.

I also work a "backup QB" section. What can we run if our QB1 gets hurt or needs to come off.

I put my false keys in here as well. Plays that would take advantage of guard readers.

Heavy goes here as well as gimmick plays we may have installed.

Creating A Call Sheet

Play Script		
Flop-Train - Cannon/Bubble	4	Palmer
RBBT GROUP - Bus Arrow JOKR	33	Duncan
Trips - Run/Screen		Palmer/Haas
R/B - Sword/Fast	11	Palmer
Bulldog - Cannon	1	Larkin
R/B - Q KNIFE	2	Jones
Bus-Arrow	1	Larkin
QUADS - 42 Fast	24	Haas
Flop - Cannon	32	Fraiser
RBBT GROUP - BUS KNIFE	2	Jones
Plays to run 1st Half		
Simpson Special	13	Shane/Fraiser
Flop - CN CRACK AND GO		Dugger
Plays for 2nd half		
Jail and Go	34	Dugger/Haas
BOGO	42	Shane
B SPECIAL	45	Larkin
BUS - STRIKER	24	Shane

NOTES FOR PLAYS-FORMATIONS

Flop - DO WE LIGHTEN THE BOX -- TRAIN??
BULLDOG -- Can we run to the Trips
JOKER-- KEYING GUARDS --
3rd Down ILB's love to blitz -- Arrow/CNN Stay/PWR
BOGO/JAIL AND GO -- Set up and throw TD's
RBBT Group -- Arrow and see how they handl motion
QB keeping off "Steal" and "Key" will be big
Ride what got us here -- but be ready to adjust

The final part of the call sheet is the opening script. I have moved to now where I will not always call these in order, but usually want to call them in the first 2 drives.

The colors correspond to our armbands that year and the last column is which player is getting the ball.

I also have a 1st half plays and 2nd half plays we wanted to run. I learned this after a few years of running everything early and not having adjustments or wrinkles for the 2nd half. These are plays you want to set up early.

Finally, I have my notes section. This is often never referred to during the game because I have memorized it.

I usually put the full chart together Sunday. I do the script on Wednesday after practice.

Creating A Call Sheet

This call sheet is available on my site: FBCoachSimpson.com or it is easy to create in excel.

Just remember the goal of a call sheet is to simplify the game for you as a play caller. Try not to put too much information on the sheet as it will make it tough to find what you need in the 10-15 seconds you have to call a play. While this call sheet works for me, you may have some additional material you wish to add.

Opening Drive

Opening Script Goals

Goals for Opening Script

-See where their eyes are – Often we use motions, false keys, play action, screen game

-Confirm alignment guesses – Use multiple sets

-Matchups – Where are we outmatched? Where are advantages?

The goals of an opening drive isn't only about scoring points and setting the tone, but also about gaining information. The hope is to confirm what you saw on film. Are they keying what you assumed they would? Are they lined up where and how you thought they would? Which players look better live than on film?

To that end I'd recommend:
1) Calling multiple formations and shifts (get to see how they align to formations and if they will shift also).

2) Using motion: Do they roll coverage or are follow or not shift?

3) Use "false keys" – Pull away from the play

Tempo

 # Tempo

My goal in tempo is to be multiple. We want to have the ability to go fast pace, but also the ability to "check with me at the line". Finally, we also want to be able to "milk the clock" if needed.

The most difficult tempo is NASCAR – This must be practiced often. Here are a few tips for NASCAR:
1) Limit formations to 1-2
2) Limit plays run to 5-6
3) Practice at end of every practice early in the season

The second tempo is "normal" for us. We want to be on the line with 20-25 seconds left on the play clock to have the ability to shift, check with me or motion.

The last tempo is our 4-minute offense. We are not in a rush, but want to be on the ball with 10 seconds on the play clock.

 # Tempo

Tempo

Types of Tempo we like
- Nascar – Limited RPO, Screens, Motions – Goal is FAST

- Base – No huddle, but often check with me or shifts/motions

- 4 Minute Offense – Still no huddle, but don't get into cadence until under 10 seconds left

**Match Tempo with ability level/philosophy
**Can change tempo from week to week – but will never "play around with very fast"

Choices in Tempo

NASCAR – If you feel you have depth or more talent than the opponent. If you had an explosive play or are sluggish on offense.

Base – Used throughout most of the game.

4 minute – End of half/game. If opponent has more talent or you are attempting to limit possessions.

Tempo

When choosing Tempo, I have found a few tips that should help in installation process:

1) Trying to work in our base is great as we can get multiple plays in a short period of time.

2) NASCAR must be worked at least once per practice if you plan to use it in the game.

3) We rarely practice slow tempo, but make sure our athletes (specifically QB) understand when we would use that tempo.

NACAR is by far the most difficult tempo to use and if you decide to make this a key fixture in the offense, I'd highly recommend that you limit formations to 1 or 2 at the most. Also, I have found it helpful to begin with a specific grouping of plays.

For example – we often work our "day 1 plays" as our NASCAR package for early season. And then slowly add if we feel we will use this package often.

If – Then
Built in Answers

If-Then

One of the reasons this offense was developed was the premise of the Wing T – IF the defense does this, THEN the offense should do this…

This premise was also big in the RPO game – that is the reason it was invented – to place players in conflict. IF the defender does this, THEN the offense runs/passes.

In any offense this should be the thought process. Have built in adjustments ready to go. This offense was designed to have these built in to any play concept we install. Having these available should provide answers for whatever the defense throws at you.

In this section I plan to go over 5 of the main "IF-THEN" questions I get asked about with this offense.

If-Then

IF we do not have a true "B" in our program

THEN:
1) We run "bypass" and "dubs" on buck sweep.

2) Put a more athletic player at this position and highlight our Jet/Counter game.

3) Run "Mustang Package" – or 2 back looks.

4) Ask him to only block second level – Belly, Insert on DUO, Bypass on Buck.

5) Roar/Lion becomes a great formation for us.

If-Then

IF we don't have a dual threat QB (more of a passer)

THEN:

1) We prefer to use the "Peak" RPO and Quick game concepts off our running game.

2) Use "Mustang" package to attack the weak side of the defense in the running game.

3) More screens will be thrown to take the place of QB running game.

4) We will practice our "HEAVY" set more often for short yardage and utilize it much more.

5) Use more drop back passing game – and "slow screens" to our RB.

 # If-Then

IF we do not have a true QB in our program

THEN:
1) Put your best athlete at QB

2) Highlight the RPO packages

3) Use a lot of Empty sets and run the QB with simple screens/quick game concepts

4) Roll out series will be a much quicker read – If ___ is not open THEN run the ball

5) Use your QB in the Heavy package

6) Be sure to develop 2-3 QB's as running them may lead to injuries

If-Then

IF the defense loads the box

THEN:
1) QB runs to gain numbers

2) Play-action game

3) Throw screens/quick game on early down

4) Bus motion – Chute route should be open

5) Start in Empty sets and motion to run the ball

If-Then

IF the offense is having a hard time with penetration

THEN:
1) Cut the splits of the offensive linemen down

2) Run Belly series more and try to get double teams

3) Screen game should be available

4) Roll QB out in the passing game with jet motion

5) Hard count or quick count to slow down the defensive line

Conclusion

Conclusion

I want to thank you for your support of my materials. This offense has served me well for many years, but like any offense it needs to continue to grow and evolve. So use this book as a guide and please reach out to let me know how it is going at your school if you choose to install it.

The coaching community is a great community to be a small part of and I am beyond surprised with the response I have received.

For those of you interested:

The entire system can be found on coachtube.com:

There is also more information on my website fbcoachsimpson.com:

Feel free to also reach out with questions:
FBCoachSimpson@gmail.com

About The Author

Coach Simpson is currently the Head Football Coach at Searcy High School, a 6A school in Arkansas. Before taking the job at Searcy, Simpson was the Head Football Coach at Southside High School, a 4A school in Arkansas. Taking over a program that had won eight games in five seasons and had been on a 20+ game losing streak, Simpson led Southside to the playoffs for four-consecutive seasons and won two conference titles in the last three seasons. For his efforts, he was named 4A-2 Conference Coach of the Year (2017), named to the as a finalist for Hooten's Coach of the Year (2017) and has been the All-Star Nominee for the 4A-2 (2016 and 2019).

This is Coach Simpson's 6th book. He was a best-selling author for his first work Find a Way: What I Wish I'd Known When I Became a Head Football Coach. The book was released in 2019 and is available on FBCoachSimpson.com. It has sold over 2300 copies as of 2020. This is the third book in the GUN-T-RPO offensive system.

About The Author

Simpson raised over $1.5 million for Southside during his 9 seasons and has overseen several major facility projects including: new field turf, expansion to fieldhouse, expansion to the school's home bleachers, and the addition of a press box and a new video-board.

Prior to Southside, Simpson took over as Head Coach at Alabama Christian Academy in Montgomery, Alabama. During his tenure there, Simpson took over a team that had been 4-18 and led them to their first home playoff game in over 20-years. For his efforts, he was named Montgomery Advertiser's All-Metro Coach of the Year as well as being voted 4A Region 2 Coach of the Year (2010). Simpson also served as the head track coach at ACA and led the girl's and boy's teams to multiple top 10 finishes in 4A.

About The Author

Simpson began his coaching career at Madison Academy, in Huntsville, Alabama. He served as a junior high basketball and football coach before working into a varsity coaching role in football. He graduated from Harding University in 2003. He is married to Jamey and has three children: Avery, Braden and Bennett. The couple was married in 2001 after meeting at Harding University.

Contact Coach Simpson

@FBCoachSimpson – Twitter
Kenny Simpson – Facebook
FBCoachSimpson.com